Christmas 2001

The Sacred Gift

ISBN: 1 86476 120 2

Unit 2, 1 Union Street, Stepney, South Australia, 5069.

This edition for
SELECT EDITIONS
Devizes
Wiltshire, UK

The Sacred Gift

Compiled and illustrated by

Peter Dunn

The Sacred Gift

Words of wisdom
handed down
speak to each generation.
They call forth
what is best in us
and touch the human heart.
They are a sacred gift...
an inheritance for
tomorrow's children,
and their dreams.

Earth

The sky is everlasting
And the earth is very old.
Why so? Because the world
Exists not for itself;
It can and will live on.

Buddhist Philosophy

We always prayed to what we took.
Before cutting down a tree, we'd say
"Forgive us, understand that we
need your warmth." That's what my
father taught me.

Marie Smith
Eyak Tribe : Native Alaskan

One day I asked my mother,
'Where is my dreaming place?'
And she took me up in the hills
and showed me a waterfall.
And then she told me,
'That is your dreaming place.
When you die
you will go back in there...
You will be in that waterfall,
watching the seasons
come and go
like your spiritual ancestors...

...In that place
you will be part of the land.
That is why we teach you
not to harm
or even mark the land.
That would be like doing harm
to yourself.
We do not own the land-
the land owns us.'

Australian Aboriginal
Bujalung Tribe

I feel it with my body
and with my blood.
Feeling all these trees...
all this country.
When the wind blows
you can feel it.
You can look, but with feeling...
that puts you out there...
in the open spaces.

Bill Neidjie
Kakadu Aborigine

The land is our provider,
our healer, and our inspiration.
It is who we are.
Every lake, every creek,
every hill, every mountain ridge
is a part of who we are.
Without the land
we would be nothing.
To survive,
we must bring the young people
onto the land.

Chief Billy Diamond
Cree Native American

Long ago they say, there was a time
when all creatures spoke the same
language. In that distant time,
the caribou and the Gwich'in
people were one. As they evolved
into separate beings, every caribou
kept a bit of caribou heart.
In this way, the caribou and Gwich'in
would always be able to sense
each other's thoughts
and feelings.

Art Davidson
Endangered Peoples

Blessing of the moon

When I see the new moon
It becomes me to lift mine eye,
It becomes me to bend my knee,
It becomes me to bow my head.

Giving thee praise,
Thou moon of guidance,
That I have seen thee again,
That I have seen the new moon,
The lovely leader of the way.

Many a one has passed beyond
In the time between the two moons,
Though I am still enjoying earth,
Thou moon of moons and of blessings.

Celtic Prayer
The Little Book of Celtic Blessings

They are
alive and holy
the stars
I gaze at from afar
but also
the earth
that I tread
the air
that I breathe,
and the light
enfolding me!

Dom Helder Camara

The earth is a sacred vessel
Of spider webs and the wings of
butterflies.
If you try to use it ,
You will crush it.
If you try to change it ,
It will shatter.
If you let it go,
It will remain useful.
If you leave it alone,
It will change for you.
Try to possess it,
And it will slip
from your grasp.

Taoist Philosophy

Gift

A civilization flourishes when people
plant trees under whose shade
they will never sit.

Greek Proverb

The wise man chooses to be last
And so becomes the first of all ;
Denying self he too is saved.
For does he not fulfillment find
In being an unselfish man?

Buddhist Philosophy

Even the milk from our own animals does not belong to us. We must give to those who need it, for a poor man shames us all.

Gabra Elder
Pastoral Nomads, Kenya

Use what talents
you possess.
The woods
will be very silent
if no birds sing
except those
which sing the best.

Henry Van Dyke

You give but little
when you give of your possessions.
It is when you give of yourself
that you truly give.
There are those who give little
of the much which they have-
and they give it for recognition
and their hidden desire makes
their gifts unwholesome.

There are those that give with joy,
and that joy is their reward.
And there are those who give with pain,
and that pain is their baptism...

...And there are those who give
and know not pain in giving,
nor do they seek joy, nor give
with mindfulness of virtue ;
They give as in yonder valley
the myrtle breathes its fragrance
into space.
Through the hands
of such as these
God speaks,
and from behind their eyes
He smiles upon the earth.

Kahlil Gibran

If thou hast two coins
with one buy bread,
with the other,
flowers for the soul.

Persian Saying

Heart

The Nyinba people, of Nepal,
have no word for love.
They call it
"beautiful from the heart."

David Maybury-Lewis
Millennium

We may be subject to many
losses in our life,
but a compassionate attitude
is something that we can always
carry with us.

Dalai Lama

Nothing
is so strong
as gentleness;
nothing is so
gentle as real
strength.

St Francis de Sales

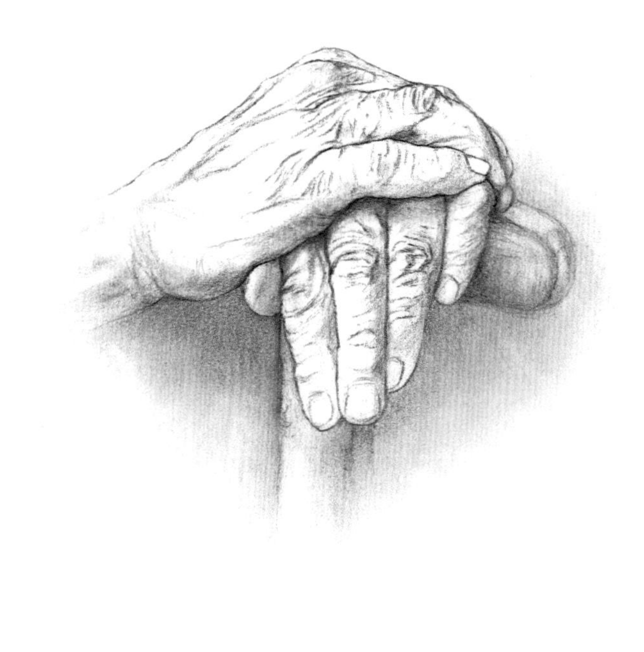

How far you go in life
depends on your being
tender with the young,
compassionate with the aged,
sympathetic with the striving, and
tolerant of the weak and strong;
because someday in your life,
you will have been all of these.

George Washington Carver

If you have
a thousand reasons
for living,
if you never feel alone,
if you wake up
wanting to sing,
if everything
speaks to you,
from the stone
in the road
to the star in the sky...

..from the loitering lizard
to the fish,
lord of the sea,
if you understand
the winds
and listen to the silence,
rejoice,
for love walks with you,
he is your comrade,
is your brother!

Dom Helder Camara

Love alone can unite living beings
so as to complete and fulfill them...
for it alone joins them
by what is deepest
in themselves.

All we need is to imagine
our ability to love developing
until it embraces
the totality of men
and of the earth.

Teilhard De Chardin

You cannot
shake hands
with
a clenched fist.

Indira Ghandi

I want to ask
other peoples of the world
to respect their ancestors.
When you know your ancestors,
you respect yourself.

Amaru
Descendant of Inca peoples

Children

When you hold the hand of your child
the Gods will bless you both.

Chinese Wisdom

Many things we need
can wait.
The child cannot.
Now is the time
his bones are being formed.
His blood is being made;
his mind is being developed.
To him we cannot say
tomorrow.
His name is today.

Gabriela Mistral

Your children are not your children.
They are the sons and daughters
of Life's longing for itself...
You may give them
your love
but not your thoughts,
For they have
their own thoughts...
You may house their bodies
but not their souls,
For their souls dwell
in the house
of tomorrow...

...You are the bows from which
your children
as living arrows are sent forth.
Let your bending
in the Archer's hand
be for gladness ;
For even as He loves
the arrow that flies,
so He loves also
the bow
that is stable.

Kahlil Gibran

Before you were conceived
I wanted you
Before you were born
I loved you
Before you were here an hour
I would die for you
This is the miracle of life.

Maureen Hawkins
The Miracle

Children are the fruit
of the seeds
of all your finest hopes.

Gloria Gaither

For out of nothingness we are not born,
and into nothingness we do not die.
Existence is a circle, and we err
when we assign to it for measurement
the limits of the cradle and the grave.

Manuel Acuna

Wisdom

Not I,
but the world says it;
All is one.

Hericlitus

Never does Nature say one thing
and wisdom another.

Juvenal

When I was young and free
and my imagination had no limits,
I dreamed of changing the world.
As I grew older and wiser,
I discovered the world
would not change,
so I shortened my sights somewhat
and decided to change
only my country.
But it too seemed immovable.
As I grew into my twilight years,
in one last desperate attempt,
I settled for changing my family,
but alas, they would have none of it.

And now, as I lie on my deathbed,
I suddenly realise;
If I had changed myself first,
then by example
I might have changed my family.
From their inspiration
and encouragement
I would then have been able
to better my country
and who knows, I may even have
changed the world.

Tomb inscription in the crypts of
Westminster Abbey, 1100 AD

The snow goose
need not bathe
to make itself white.

Neither need you
do anything
but be yourself.

Lao-Tzu

There is nothing at all
on this earth that is not paired.
Everything must have
its counterpart.
The right hand is not worth much
without the left hand.
You must work to put everything
in order, in balance.
You must work especially
to overcome one's debt to death
and one's debt to life –
for they too are a pair.

Wisdom of Yekuana people, Venezuela

Those who are unafraid to say
they do not know
become wise.
Those who insist they know
never learn.
Those who pay attention
to their weaknesses
gain strength.
Wisdom and strength
come from the courage
to see things as they are.

Taoist Philosophy

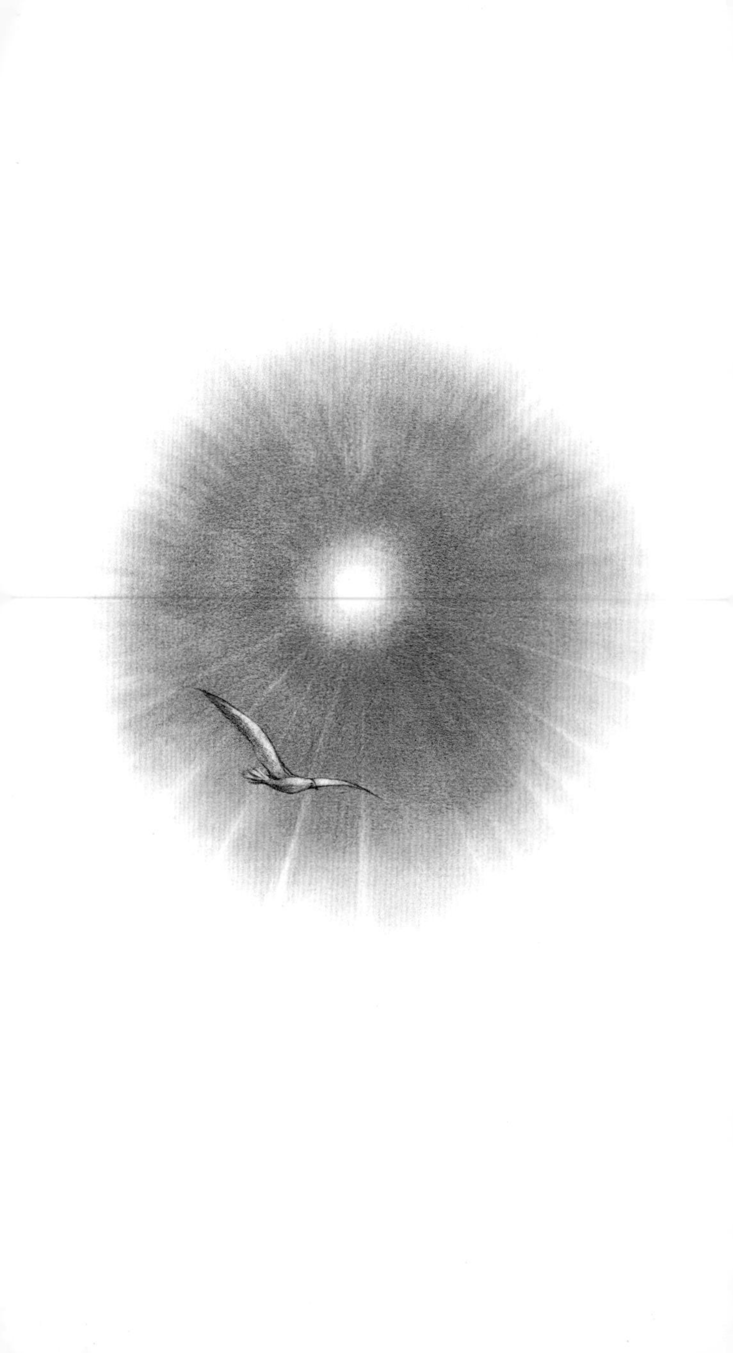

May the nourishment
of the earth be yours,
may the clarity of light be yours,
may the fluency of the ocean be yours,
may the protection of the ancestors
be yours...
And may a slow wind
work these words of love around you,
an invisible cloak to mind your life.

Celtic Blessing
Anam Cara